Genesis

Chapters 1, 2 and 3

By Charles Ozanne

ISBN: 978-1-78364-640-1

First published in 2020

www.obt.org.uk

****

THE OPEN BIBLE TRUST
Fordland Mount, Upper Basildon,
Reading, RG8 8LU, UK.

Genesis Chapters 1, 2 and 3

Contents

Introduction

The first chapter of Genesis is a chapter of immense and abiding interest to Christian believers. I hope to give a simple straightforward explanation without any frills (or thrills, though Bible truth is always thrilling!). Questions of science I leave to one side. The chapter itself should be sufficient answer to such matters. Here at least we have the truth, God's version of how the world came into being, a marvellous divine creation in the not so distant past.

The first verse of Genesis is without question the most remarkable combination of seven words that has ever been written. Here we have God's stamp of authorship, His imprimatur, on the Bible as a whole. I refer to the numerical design underlying this verse. It is not my purpose to indulge my penchant for Bible Numerics at this time, but I cannot resist pointing out (for those who don't already know) the breath-taking numerical structure which stares one in the face when the Hebrew text of this verse is examined. (For more on this see the Appendix: *The Numerics of Genesis 1:1*).

Genesis 1:1-2:3

In the beginning: Genesis 1:1-2

How then do we understand the first verse of Genesis? Many would say it speaks of God's initial act of creation, a creation which brought the world into existence but in an unformed and empty condition as described in the second verse.

A popular version of this is offered by the Gap Theory. According to the Gap Theory there is a gap of many thousands of years between the first and second verses of Genesis. During this interval, it is argued, all the geological ages and fossils may be conveniently placed without contradicting anything the Bible says. This period, it is claimed, concluded with a cataclysm or judgment (connected possibly with Satan's eviction from heaven) in which the earth was reduced to the state of *tohu wa-bohu*, waste and void, of verse 2. Thereafter a re-creation followed, the six-day event of Genesis One when the earth was restored to the state of excellence which God originally intended.

A strong advocate of this theory (among others) is Sidlow Baxter in his useful introduction *Explore the Book*, and is adopted by Bullinger whose note on Genesis 1:1 in *The Companion Bible* says, "Creation in eternity past to which all fossils and remains belong." This was very popular in the last century, but today it is losing ground as more and more people realise that the Bible teaches no such thing. It is a classic example of *eisergesis*, reading into the Bible something that is not there, as opposed to *exergesis*, drawing out from the Bible what is really there. There are today better ways of explaining the findings of palaeontology without resorting to fanciful theories to which the Bible lends no support.

Advocates of the Gap Theory tells us with an air of confidence that the second verse should be translated "And the earth *became* waste and void", on the analogy of Genesis 19:26, "she (Lot's wife) *became* a pillar of salt." But the construction there is different. If that were the meaning intended the writer would have expressed himself differently. The Gap Theory provides a convenient dumping ground for all the inconvenient discoveries of modern science, but like most other theories it fails to provide a satisfactory answer.

Several other *Theories of Creation*[1] are ably set out by Sylvia Penny in her booklet on the subject (OBT, 1998).

---

[1] Details of *Theories of Creation* by Sylvia Penny are given at the end of this book.

However, human theories are confusing and generally unhelpful. The Bible is our only source of authoritative information, so to that we now turn.

A more correct view

A better way to view Genesis 1:1 is to see it as a heading or title. It introduces the work of creation which follows (Genesis 1:2-2:3) and sums up its contents. One pointer in that direction are the words "God created" in Genesis 2:3. This verse says literally,

"And God blessed the seventh day and sanctified it because in it he ceased from all his work which *God created* to make."

The words "God created" are quoted from the first verse, and they refer here to all God's work of creation as detailed in the previous chapter. This, I submit, is its meaning in the first verse as well.

In the next verse also, 2:4, all the important words of Genesis 1:1 are repeated. 1:1 has seven words but two of them are simply the untranslatable *eth* that precedes the definite object. There are therefore five meaningful words in 1:1:

In the beginning, created, God, the heavens, the earth.

These are all repeated in 2:4:

These are the generations of *the heavens* and *the earth* when they were *created, in the day* (corresponding to *In the beginning*) that the Lord *God* made earth and heavens.

This new section of Genesis, of which 2:4 is the heading, describes what resulted from the creation of the heavens and earth just described.

How the narrative begins

Hence we regard the first verse of Genesis as the title to what follows in 1:2 to 2:3. The narrative proper begins at verse 2. Here the writer makes it clear that *the earth* is what interests him most: the narrative that follows is decidedly geocentric. "Now the earth was without form and empty ..." This is the way that narratives often begin in the Bible. It is the way chapter 3 begins: "Now the serpent was more crafty ..." And chapter 4 as well though the verb is different: "Now the man knew his wife ..."

In 1:2 the earth is described as "without form and empty." These words should not be understood as shameful or suspicious. The earth at this stage was certainly deficient but it was not defective. It was like an unborn child swimming in a dark and watery world waiting to be born.

This is how the earth was "in the beginning". Not only was it without form and empty, it was also covered with water, water that reached to the sky in the form of mist indistinguishable from the water itself. And what is more, there was total darkness. No day or night, no sun or moon, no dry land or air to breathe, certainly no habitat for life of any kind! So it is written in Psalm 104:5-6: "He set the earth on its foundation, so that it should never be moved. You covered it with the deep as with a garment; the waters stood above the mountains."

All the while, however, "the Spirit of God was hovering over the face of the waters." The Spirit was hovering like an eagle "hovers (or flutters) over its young, spreading out its wings ..." (Deuteronomy 32:11). As in the New Testament, it is often difficult to decide when the Spirit is a Person or a spiritual force sent by God. But here it certainly reads like a Person. In fact, the Trinity is suggested in the opening verse where we have Elohim, God, a plural word coupled with a singular verb, and here we have the Spirit! The stage is now set for the first day.

The First Day: Genesis 1:3-5

"And God said, Let there be Light!" Immediately light flooded the world, and God saw that it was good. The word 'good' has many shades of meaning: beautiful, attractive, desirable, excellent, wonderful. The light created on the first day was all of these, but how come there was light at all before the creation of the sun on the fourth day? No problem at all! In the New Jerusalem "they will need no light of lamp or *sun*, for the Lord God will be their light" (Revelation 22:5). That is how it was in the beginning. The world was bathed in supernatural divine light. And that should not surprise us seeing that God is Light (1 John 1:5), and the Lord Jesus said, "I am the Light of the world" (John 8:12).

After that God proceeded to separate the light from the darkness. The light He called Day and the darkness He called Night. But how could there be day and night without the sun and moon? Again, no problem! For the first three days this divine light fulfilled all the functions of the sun and moon until, on the fourth day, this source of light was superseded by the sun and moon. In any case, a day is the time it takes the earth to rotate on its axis, and this takes place independently of the sun. There could not have been a "day one" at all unless day and night had already been established.

Yom and Laylah

This naming of the Day and Night, and the other namings mentioned in this record, must have occurred later on since there was no one in existence for God to speak to prior to the creation of Adam and Eve, and no language at all in current use. This naming is placed here for convenience.

Why, we may ask, did God use the particular sounds Yom and Laylah for Day and night? The answer is, we don't know. But presumably these words conveyed a meaning which suited the phenomena being described. They must have had a primeval meaning prior to their present assignment. Language of course changes quite rapidly over time. The language spoken by Adam and Eve was certainly very different from the Hebrew spoken by Moses two and a half thousand years later. Clearly the language has been updated. Even that spoken by Moses would have been 'archaic' compared with that spoken by Ezra a thousand years on when the Old Testament assumed its present shape. Hence it is futile debating how words were used in that remote time! All we need know is that the Hebrew text in front of us is the divinely-inspired and numerically-authenticated text!

There was evening and there was morning

One small point remains. Did the day begin in the morning or the evening? From the fact that evening is mentioned first it might appear that the day began in the evening. But it seems more likely that the opposite was the case. The word translated 'was' is the form of the verb often translated 'and it came to pass'. In other words, the evening came to pass (when the day terminated) and the morning came to pass (when the night terminated). In 1:5 the Day is mentioned before the Night, and the same is true in verses 14 and 16. It is more natural to think of the day as preceding the night and this, it seems, is the usual order in the Bible.

It is however stipulated that certain feasts should start in the evening prior to the official day by way of preparation. For example, the feast of Unleavened Bread was to begin "on the fourteenth day of the month at evening" (Exodus 12:18). It was to begin in the evening prior to the fifteenth, but the day is still called the fourteenth. The same applies to the Day of Atonement. It was to begin in the evening prior to the tenth day of the month (Leviticus 23:32), but the day is still called the ninth, not the tenth.

There was now, at the end of the first day, day and night, but there was still no dry land or air to breathe. The darkness had been assigned to its proper place, but the earth was still without form and empty, and water covered the earth. It covered the highest mountain and reached to the sky in the form of watery mist.

The Second Day: Genesis 1:6-8

"And God said, Let there be an expanse in the midst of the waters, and let it separate the waters from the waters." As is usual in this chapter God first says what He is going to do (v.6) and then does it using the same or similar language (v.7). Here we have another separation, the separation of the waters under the expanse from the waters above the expanse.

The expanse (or firmament) is here the space between the earth and the sky. It has the same meaning in verse 20 where the birds fly across the expanse of the heavens. In verses 14, 15 and 17, however, the same word is applied to the astral heavens where the sun, moon and stars are situated.

The word means something spread out, either by stretching like a tent or by hammering as of metal on a solid surface. Elihu combines both ideas in Job 37:18: "Can you, like him, *spread out* the skies, hard as a cast-metal mirror?" In Psalm 136:6 it is the earth which is spread out: "To him who *spread out* the earth above the waters, for his steadfast love endures for ever." Using another verb of similar meaning, God stretches out the heavens in Job 9:8 and Jeremiah 10:12.

And it was so

A better translation would be "And it was accomplished (or established)." The word *so* is derived from a stem meaning "to be firm."

The heavens

The expanse is now given a name: God called it "Heavens". The word *Shamayim* probably means something high or lifted up. This word also is used in more than one sense. Here it refers to the space between the earth and the sky, and it has this meaning in verses 20,26,28 and 30, where reference is made to "the birds of the heavens" and "the expanse of the heavens" where the birds fly. In verses 14,15 and 17 however the same expression "the expanse of the heavens" is applied to the astral heavens where the sun and moon are located.

It is not said of the second day that God saw it was good since nothing new was made on the second day. Now the vault of the heavens is magnificently stretched out as far as the eye can see. Above it are the upper waters still intact, and below are the waters under the expanse, the vast ocean which still covered the earth.

Some would say the upper waters stayed there until the Flood when the windows of heaven were opened and the waters came down. But this is disproved by Psalm 148:4-6 where reference is made to "the waters above the heavens." It says there, "he established them for ever and ever; he gave a decree, and it shall not pass away." So these waters are still there, it seems, in the form of clouds. It did not rain before the fall of Adam and Eve. After that it did rain but the water canopy remained intact.

The Third Day: Genesis 1:9-13

For the third day two creative acts are recorded. First the water which still covered the entire world is gathered into one place allowing the dry land to appear. This would suggest that all the continents were connected at that time, one huge land-mass surrounded by the turbulent ocean. This situation was destroyed beyond repair by the Flood though one can still see how the continents might once have fitted together. The animals migrating to Noah's ark would have had no seas to cross. Impelled by a God-given instinct they would have known where to go and how long it would take! Even after the Flood there must have been land bridges so that the animals could return to their original habitats.

Once more the Lord gives names to the dry land and the sea, though again it is not clear why He chose the particular phonemes *erets* and *yammim*. They must have conveyed an appropriate meaning.

Plant life

Secondly, the land is immediately covered with plants of various kinds. "God said, Let the earth sprout sprouts (or vegetate vegetation)." More elegantly, "Let the earth be covered with a fresh green mantle of verdure." This is followed by two categories of plant: smaller plants yielding seed and fruit trees bearing fruit containing seeds. These same two categories are mentioned in verse 29 as food suitable for human consumption. We are thinking therefore of cereal crops such as wheat and barley along with fruit trees of various kinds. These are singled out as of special significance though presumably other varieties of plant were also created.

Kinds

Here for the first time we encounter the phrase "after their kind." It is not entirely clear what is covered by the term *kind* (genus, species, family), but whatever is meant the boundaries between them can never be crossed. Hybrids, artificially created by human ingenuity, have no stability or permanence. Left to themselves they either die out or revert to type very quickly.

The Fourth Day: Genesis 1:14-19

The fourth day of creation corresponds to the first. On the first day light was created, on the fourth day lights in the expanse of the heavens. Their purpose was primarily to separate the day from the night, though also for other purposes – signs and seasons, days and years.

Interest focuses on the two great lights: the greater light to rule the day and the lesser light to rule the night, and it adds, almost as an afterthought, "and the stars"! There is no emphasis on the universe as such which excites in us so much admiration and amazement. It is only mentioned in passing since its impact on the earth is small compared to the sun and moon.

The light created on the first day "separated the light from the darkness" (v.4). That source of light is now superseded by the sun and moon whose function also is "to separate the light from the darkness" (v.18). The two lights are not given names in this instance, possibly because the sun and moon were worshipped by the heathen and it was not thought appropriate to mention the names of heathen gods.

Why, we may ask, didn't God create the sun and moon on the first day instead of creating two sources of light both fulfilling the same function? The reason, surely, was to prove to the world that the sun and moon are only secondary sources of light, and dispensable at that. Far more brilliant is God's supernatural effulgence of light as manifested on the first day. It is therefore He who is to be worshipped, not the sun, moon and stars.

Signs and seasons

As for the secondary purposes of the sun and moon "for signs and for seasons, for days and years", we think especially of Luke 21:25: "And there will be signs in the sun, moon and stars" prior to the return of the Son of Man; also, Matthew 24:29 and Joel 2:31. There is however a warning in Jeremiah 10:2 not to be dismayed by the signs of the heavens, "because the heathen are dismayed at them." Comets, eclipses, blue moons and the like should not concern us unduly. But in the days preceding the return of the Lord there will be unusual signs in the heavens. We cannot say what form they will take, but presumably they will be clearly recognizable as such.

One such sign of this kind may be that seen by John in Revelation 12:1. He saw what is called a great sign in heaven, "a woman clothed with the sun, with the moon under her feet, and on her head a crown of twelve stars." And again in 12:3 and 15:1.

Genesis Chapters 1, 2 & 3   Page 24

Was the universe there already?

According to Herbert C Leupold, in his *Exposition of Genesis*, the heavenly bodies were already in existence prior to the fourth day. But the Word says God *made* them (v.16). He also *made* the expanse (7), the beasts of the earth (25), man (26), everything (31). There is a subtle difference between *make* and *create*, which we will examine in the next article. But the two words are almost synonymous and are often used in parallel expressions (1:21,25; 1:26,27; 2:3; 2:4; 1:27 with 9:6).

Make does not necessarily mean to make out of nothing at all since Adam was made out of the dust of the ground (2:7), and the same is doubtless true of the animals and plants. Even the stars may have been made out of cosmic dust, though that too must have been created by God. But we can say with confidence that what was made was something entirely new. The finished product bore no resemblance to the material it was made of.

How long is a day?

We can however agree with Leupold who comments as follows on the words evening and morning:

"It is the author's purpose by this means, emphatically to declare the six days alike as to length and general character – regular 24 hour days."

These "days" are clearly presented as literal days: evening-morning, day and night, the sun to rule the day and the moon to rule the night. These expressions make no sense if literal days are not intended – not to mention Exodus 20:11 and 31:17 where we are told in so many words that "in six days the Lord made heaven and earth."

The Fifth Day: Genesis 1:20-23

The fifth day corresponds to the second. On the second day God made the expanse in the midst of the waters, and now on the fifth day He creates the birds that fly across the expanse, and the fish which teem in the waters.

In verse 11 God had said "Let the earth sprout sprouts." Here (v.20) He says, "Let the waters swarm swarms (or teem teems) of living soul." Living soul, *nephesh hayyah*, is also applied to mammals and reptiles (24), and indeed to every living creature in which there is *nephesh hayyah* (30), including man (2:7). Man and beast do not differ greatly in their physical make-up. They are all living souls, they are all made of dust or slime, and they all return to dust when they die. It is only in the spiritual sphere that man has the advantage. Only mankind has the ability to communicate with God, to obey or disobey His commands, to worship and adore Him. Only to man has God entrusted His written word and given the certain hope of resurrection and eternal life.

Create

In verse 21 the word "created" is found. This is its first occurrence after verse 1, and it is used again only of man (v.27, three times). Ask the average person what is the most wonderful thing that God has created and he will probably say, the solar system along with the rolling galaxies and their myriads of stars. No one can deny that the universe is a marvel beyond belief, but in Genesis 1 there is no emphasis on the universe. It is simply dismissed in two words, *and the stars!* Far more wonderful in the eyes of the writer is the creation of the sea creatures and the birds. Why should that be? It is of course the creation of LIFE which is so amazing. Scientists speak as if life just happens when the conditions are right. Nothing could be further from the truth! It involved a very special act of God to bring life into existence. Cassuto says:

Bara, create, is only used when Scripture wishes to stress the *wonder* of something,
whereas *Asah,* make, points to the making of something that did not exist before.

And Leupold:

An entirely new type of being has come into existence, creatures that move and are animate … a monumental epoch-making achievement that deserves … the verb 'and He created'.

Yes, the smallest fish or bird is more wonderful than the universe, simply because *it lives!*

God's blessing

"God blessed them, saying, Be fruitful and multiply and fill the waters in the seas, and let birds multiply on earth." This is the first of three blessings. In verse 28 Adam and Eve are blessed in similar terms, and in 2:3 God blesses the seventh day.

The Sixth Day: Genesis 1:24-31

Like the third day the sixth is in two parts. The third day saw the emergence of the Earth, and now the earth brings forth *nephesh hayyah*, living soul or soul of life, according to their kinds. Three classes of living soul are mentioned: domestic animals or cattle, creeping animals, and wild animals. These may well include all the living creatures that inhabit the earth, with the exception of fish and birds already mentioned. Also made on this day were dinosaurs and other large animals that perished in the Flood.

Kinds

"After their kinds" occurs ten times in this chapter, and five of them are in verses 24 and 25. It occurs also three times in verses 11-12 of plants and trees, and twice in verse 21 of fish and birds. It could not be emphasized more strongly that every species of plant and living creature is strictly defined and segregated one from another. Any suggestion that one animal (or plant) has evolved into another is powerfully excluded. However, it does not rule out the adaptation of plants and animals to environmental pressures and conditions which may result in substantive changes in appearance and habit. All the fauna in the world today are descended from those rescued from oblivion in Noah's ark.

Man

Created on the third day were the cereal plants and fruit trees suitable for human consumption. Now on the sixth day the man and woman are created who will benefit from this provision. Man is duly created in the image of God and after His likeness, and they (mankind) are given dominion over the fish and birds, the livestock, and indeed all the earth including every creeping thing that creeps on the earth. Virtually the same authority is given to Noah in Genesis 9:2.

An incredible amount seems to take place on the sixth day: the creation of the animal kingdom, the creation of man, the planting of the garden in Eden, the cultivation of pleasant trees, man's placement in the garden, man's naming of all the beasts of the field and birds of heaven, the making and naming of the Woman (Gen. 1:24-31; 2:7-25). Is it possible that all this took place in a single day? It could have, I suppose, but I am inclined to think that in fact it took several days or even a week or two. For convenience it is bunched together in a single day, rather like the naming of the light and darkness on the first day probably took place after the creation of Adam and Eve.

God's Image

God made man in His own image (26,27). But Adam fathered a son in his own likeness, after *his* image (5:3). The sad truth is that Adam and Eve, though created in the image of God, lost God's image when they fell, and ever since men have fathered children in their own image.

The good news is that God's image is restored in Christ. Christ is "the image of the invisible God" (Colossians 1:15), "the exact imprint of his nature" (Hebrews 1:3). That image is now being formed in us (in a derivative sense) as we grow in grace and the knowledge of the Lord.

Romans 8:29: "For those whom he foreknew he also predestined to be conformed to the image of His Son, in order that he might be the firstborn among many brothers." 2 Corinthians 3:18: "We all, with unveiled face, beholding the glory of the Lord, are being transformed into the same image from one degree of glory to another." Colossians 3:9-10: You have put off the old man with its practices and have put on the new man, which is being renewed in knowledge after the image of its Creator."

Food

Man is given two classes of food, herbs yielding seed and fruit trees which have seed-bearing fruit, the same as those mentioned in verses 11-12. Meat is not permitted until after the Flood (9:3). Nothing is said about animal products such as milk and cheese, eggs and honey. These may have been left to fulfil their primary function. Alternatively, Adam and Eve may have been given a free hand to choose for themselves in borderline matters such as this.

The animals are given a wider diet: every green plant, but even they were herbivores and remained so until the Flood. And such they will be again when the Lord returns to establish His Kingdom here on earth (Isaiah 11:6-9; 65:25).

The Creation is now complete. The Lord surveyed everything He had made and pronounced it *"very* good." It was not just good but very good, excellent to a superlative degree! And here ended *the* sixth day. Only the sixth and seventh days have *the* attached to mark their special significance.

Us and Our

One more observation before we leave this chapter. Here we encounter for the first time the phenomenon of the Divine 'we' ('us' or 'our'). In verse 26 God said, "Let *us* make man in *our* image, after *our* likeness." Other examples are 3:22 "Behold the man has become like one of *us*"; 11:7 "Let *us* go down, and there let *us* confuse their language"; Isaiah 6:8 "Whom shall I send, and who will go for *us*?"

Some would say that this is the Royal We as when Queen Victoria said "We are not amused!" or that God takes counsel with His angels. The Royal We is used by the Persian king Artaxerxes in Ezra 4:18 but never by a Hebrew king. According to Cassuto it is "the plural of exhortation", as when David said, "Let us fall into the hand of the Lord, for his mercy is great" (2 Samuel 24:14). But David here includes all those who would suffer with him, and the other suggestions are not attested.

In Genesis 1:26-27 *our* and *his* are used interchangeably. Verse 26, "Let us make man in *our* image"; but verse 27, "God created man in *his* own image", and 9:6, "God made man in *his* own image." And the same applies in Isaiah 6:8 quoted above. We have already noticed a plurality in the Godhead in the first two verses of Genesis: the plural Elohim with a singular verb, and the personal Spirit of God. The same plurality seems to be implied in the *his/our, I/us* phenomenon. Here we have the Divine We, a plurality in the Godhead better known as the Trinity.

The Seventh Day: Genesis 2:1-3

We have reached the seventh day all too quickly! In most versions Genesis 2 begins, "Thus the heavens and the earth were finished, and all the host of them." The word *Thus* gives the line a backward look, a glance back to what God had already done in the previous six days. It should therefore be the last verse in chapter One, not the first verse in chapter Two. The Masoretes however knew better than the KJV translator and all his slavish followers. The word *Thus* is not in the Hebrew, and this verse looks forward not backward. It introduces the seventh day as shown by the fact that the word "finished" is repeated in the next verse.

When the same word is found in successive verses it is obviously deliberate, and it must accordingly be translated in the same way. This is done in the ESV but many versions do not. The KJV has "finished in verse 1 and "ended" in verse 2; the NIV "completed" in verse 1 and "finished" in verse 2. This is because they misunderstand verse 1 as looking backward. The seventh day follows the pattern of the previous days. First God states what He is going to do (or in this case what He has done) and then proceeds to do it, using the same or similar words.

What did God do?

What therefore did God do on the seventh day? Three things are mentioned:

God finished on the seventh day his work which he made
He rested (ceased) on the seventh day from all his work which he made
God blessed the seventh day and sanctified it because in it he ceased from all his work which God created to make.

In all three the words "seventh day", "his work", and "made" or "make" are mentioned. The word for "work" is *melakhah*, skilled work, as opposed to *avodah*, unskilled work. No one can deny that creating the world involved amazing skill though to God it was all in a day's work!

God finished His work

So was there something more to do? Some finishing touches maybe, a rogue star shooting off course or a bewildered hedgehog not quite sure what to do next? Of course not! God had already pronounced everything "very good". What more therefore was there to do? Nothing at all, to be sure. It seems that God carried out one more inspection and then pronounced His work to be truly finished.

He rested (or ceased) from all His work

So was God tired after all His hard work and in need of a rest? Of course not; He was not in the least bit tired. He could easily have created another universe on the very next if He had wanted. The truth is the word *shabat* does not mean to rest; it means to *cease* or *desist.* So what God did when He had finished His work was simply to stop working! Some people cannot stop working. Even after they have finished they must go on working. But God is not a workaholic; when He had finished He closed His mouth and stopped!

God blessed the seventh day

Verse 3 is literally translated, "And God blessed the seventh day and sanctified it (pronounced it holy), because in it he ceased from all his work which God created to make." Cassuto explains the concluding words as "an act of creation that is also a making, that is, a wondrous work implying the making of things that never existed before." This was the only positive thing God did on the seventh day: He blessed the seventh day and sanctified it.

Is this a command to observe the Sabbath?

From the fact that God blessed the seventh day and pronounced it holy, should we conclude that Adam and Eve thereafter observed the Sabbath day? The answer is No! There is no record of any of the patriarchs observing the Sabbath day in Genesis. In fact, the word does not even occur again except once in a different context (8:22). Not until Exodus 16 do we find any directive to observe the seventh day as a day of rest.

The fact is, the patriarchs were not under law. They had freedom to rest or not to rest as and when they saw fit. But from Exodus onwards the Jews were under law as they still are. Regrettably many Christian believers put themselves under law, but that should not be the case. The apostle Paul is very clear on this point:

"Therefore let no one pass judgment on you in questions of food and drink, or with regard to a festival or a new moon or a Sabbath." (Colossians 2:16)

"For he himself is our peace, who has made us both one and has broken down in his flesh the dividing wall of hostility by abolishing the law of commandments and ordinances...." (Ephesians 2:14-15)

Like the patriarchs we have freedom to do what we think appropriate. There is no law to say that we should not do the shopping on the Sabbath (Sunday for us) or hang out the laundry, and no one has the right to tell us yea or nay. Of course, we may not think it appropriate to do certain things on the Sabbath, but that is for us to decide. (Not e.g. The Lord's Day Observance Society whose well-meaning endeavours has the effect of putting people under law.)

Food and drink

The same applies to food and drink mentioned by Paul in the same verse. No restrictions were put on Noah's diet. He is permitted to eat "every moving thing that lives" in Genesis 9:3, where "all" or "everything" is the first and last word. The same applies to us. We can eat anything that takes our fancy subject to hygiene and general suitability.

No evening

There is no evening to the Seventh Day. This would suggest that the situation here described has continued ever since. In fact, the Jewish Christians addressed in Hebrews are encouraged to enter God's rest, "for we who have believed enter that rest" (4:3), and "whoever has entered God's rest has also rested from his works as God did from his" (4:10). "Be diligent therefore to enter that rest" (4:11).

Genesis 2:4-25

After the opening section, 1:1-2:3, the Book of Genesis consists of eleven *Toledoth* or generations. This word is derived from the verb *yalad*, to bear or beget. It means therefore "begettings" and points to what the subject begets or produces. Hence the section headed "the generations of Terah" is all about Terah's son Abraham, not Terah himself. Some have thought these titles are endings rather than headings, but that is clearly not the case as may be seen from the three cases outside of Genesis, Numbers 3:1, Ruth 4:18, and Matthew 1:1.

The generations of the heavens and the earth: Genesis 2:4

Genesis 2:4 introduces "the generations of the heavens and the earth when they were created", that is, what the heavens and the earth produced in the years following their creation. The whole of verse 4 constitutes this introduction, not just the first half as in the NIV.

It forms a chiasmus or introversion in which "the heavens and the earth" corresponds to "earth and heavens", and "when they were created" to "in the day that the Lord God made." Here also we have all the elements of Genesis 1:1: in the day (answering to "In the beginning"), the (Lord) God, created, the heavens, the earth. This goes to show that Genesis 1:1 is also a heading, introducing and summing up the days of creation. Genesis One describes how God created the heavens and the earth, and Genesis Two describes what was produced by this creation.

The Lord God

The combination Yahweh Elohim, Lord God, occurs here for the first time. In the first chapter it is always Elohim on its own, that is the Creator God, but in chapters 2 and 3, nineteen times, Elohim is identified with Yahweh, the familiar national Lord of the Israelites, by combining the two. This is found nowhere else in the first five books except for Exodus 9:30. According to the so-called higher critics, in their stultifying folly and blindness, the first chapter was written by P and the second chapter by a different source J or E. They then look for contradictions to justify their theory. This nonsense is rejected out of hand by Cassuto and all enlightened commentators Jewish as well as Christian.

Before and after: Genesis 2:5-6

Verses 5 tells us what was not, and verse 6 what was, before the fall of Adam and Eve. Verse 5 is best understood as an independent statement. We are here informed of two things that did not exist at that time and the reasons for their non-existence. First there was no bush of the field, by which we understand noxious plants such as thorns and thistles mentioned in 3:18, the reason being that "the Lord God had not caused it to rain on the land." And secondly, there was no plant of the field such as wheat and barley (3:18), the reason being "there was no man to work the ground." There would have been sufficient wheat growing in the fertile soil for the needs of Adam and Eve, but before the Fall there would have been no need to work the ground by manual labour and human effort.

What there was

Having told us what was not, verse 6 tells us what was at that time. But here there is a misunderstanding enshrined in most of our translations. The ESV, along with most other versions, has "mist" in the text, but in the footnote it says "spring". In the NIV it is the other way round: the text has "stream" and the footnote "mist". My Hebrew dictionary says "stream, or perhaps mist." There can be no doubt that stream or spring is the true meaning of the word, and such it is translated in both the Septuagint *(pege)* and the Vulgate *(fons)*.

No, it was not a mist that went up from the land, but a spring of water rising up from the earth. This water gushed (Hebrew, *hishqah*) over the surface of the ground refreshing everything in its path. Psalm 104 is a poetic commentary on Genesis 1 and 2. It says there in verses 10,11,16:

You make springs gush forth in the valleys;
    they flow between the hills;
    they give drink to every beast of the field;
    the wild donkeys quench their thirst ….
    The trees of the Lord are watered abundantly.

When Abraham gave Lot the choice where he should go, Lot chose the Jordan Valley because it was "well watered like the garden of the Lord, like the land of Egypt" (Genesis 13:10). What was so special about the land of Egypt? It was of course that Egypt was not dependent on rain. Egypt was (and is?) watered by the annual inundation of the Nile which flooded the Nile Delta with nutritious mud and silt year upon year without fail. The Jordan valley (before the destruction of Sodom and Gomorrah, v.10) was like that, watered by springs and streams like Egypt and the Garden of Eden.

Rain is intermittent at the best of times. There is either too much of it or too little, and it is never very pleasant. In the Garden of Eden there was a perennial supply of water gushing out of the ground. And that is how it will be in Israel in the millennium, and everywhere else in the New Earth.

Zechariah 14:8: "On that day living waters shall flow out from Jerusalem, half of them to the eastern sea and half of them to the western sea. It shall continue in summer as in winter."

Joel 3:18: "all the stream beds of Judah shall flow with water; and a fountain shall come forth from the house of the Lord and water the valley of Shitttim."

Psalm 46:4: "There is a river whose streams make glad the city of God, the holy habitation of the Most High."

Psalm 36:8-9: "you give them drink from the river of your delights (your edens!). For with you is the fountain of life; in your light do we see light."

Revelation 22:1: "the angel showed me the river of the water of life, bright as crystal, flowing from the throne of God and of the Lamb."

Man, trees and rivers: Genesis 2:7

> "Then the Lord God formed the man (*ha-adam*) of dust from the ground (*ha-adamah*), and breathed into his nostrils the breath of life, and the man became a living creature (*nephesh hayyah,* soul of life or living soul)." (Genesis 2:7)

Three things are said of the man. First, he is formed from dust or fine earth. This is the united testimony of Scripture: Genesis 3:19 ("Dust you are and to dust you shall return"); Job 33:6 ("I too was pinched from a piece of clay"). In this respect man is no different from the beasts.

Secondly, God breathed into his nostrils the breath of life. This is true of all God's creatures. Genesis 7:22, "Everything on the dry land in whose nostrils was the breath of life died." Once again man is no different from all other animate creatures.

Thirdly, he became a living soul. This is said also of the fish and the birds in 1:20-21, and of animals and reptiles in 1:24. Man therefore is no different from all other animals in his physical constitution. He does of course have a superior brain, but it is chiefly in the spiritual realm that he excels. Only man is created in the image of God (1:26-27), and only man has the prospect of eternal life in resurrection. Only man can communicate with God in prayer and consciously carry out His will in their lives.

Man however is not immortal. Even before the Fall Adam and Eve were not immortal. Quite possibly their lives would have continued indefinitely so long as they ate from the Tree of Life (cp. 3:22). But all that was now in the balance. Their future well-being depended entirely on how they would respond to the challenge which was soon to confront them.

Lots of lovely trees: 2:8-9

The Garden of Eden was situated in Eden, an area or country which gave its name to the Garden. It was also situated "in the east", by which is meant presumably east of Israel, in the vicinity of Babylon or Assyria, though the world was very different before the Flood. The Garden was defined by the Tigris and Euphrates rivers (2:14), but these rivers have changed courses since the Fall of Adam and Eve. No one knows where the Garden was situated, and in any case, it could not be found on the map of today's world.

It is emphasized that God made to spring up in the Garden "*every* tree that is pleasant to the sight and good for food." There was a super-abundance of fruit-bearing trees all of them lovely to look at as well as delicious to eat. Adam and Eve were spoilt for choice, but they could not keep their eyes off the one tree they were forbidden to eat from. That was the Tree of the Knowledge of Good and Evil which Eve found more attractive than all the rest. There were no restrictions on the Tree of Life. That tree is mentioned again in 3:22 and 24, and again in the Book of Revelation where it is restored to its former place of glory and pre-eminence (Revelation 2:7; 22:14,19).

Four rivers: 2:10-14

In verses 10 to 14 we are taken on a brief tour of the Garden of Eden. It was watered by a river which flowed into it from the country outside. Having reached the Garden it branched into four streams which took their separate courses. These rivers were called the Pishon, Gihon, Tigris and Euphrates. Only the last two are known to later times, but even they were very different from what they are today. They are now two separate rivers which rise from different sources. They both rise in the Armenian highlands not far from one another, but there is no question of them joining at any point.

The rivers Pishon and Gihon are unknown. Pishon is derived from a root meaning to jump or skip about, and Gihon to burst forth. Gihon is now known as the name of a spring in Jerusalem at the foot of the Mount of Olives, but that of course has no relevance to the Garden of Eden. In Genesis the Gihon "flowed around the whole land of Cush." Cush is normally Ethiopia though there are some who think there was another Cush further north. We are really none the wiser, the geography of the world having changed so much since the Flood.

Adam's instructions: Genesis 2:15-17

Adam was given the job of tending and keeping the Garden. This would have kept him busy without exerting himself unduly. He was told that he could eat of every tree in the Garden with one exception: the Tree of the Knowledge of Good and Evil. If he were to eat of that tree, he would die on that very day. God's prohibition admits of no uncertainty. On the day that he ate from that tree he would not simply lose his immortality, he would cease to exist.

Verse 16: "Eating you may eat" – freedom without restriction to partake of every tree in the Garden.
Verse 17: "dying you shall die" – death without mercy or delay.

A close parallel is provided by 1 Kings 2:36-46. Shimei, who cursed David, is put under house arrest by Solomon. Solomon strictly forbade him to leave Jerusalem. He said to him, "In the day [the same as in Genesis] you go out and cross the brook Kidron, know for certain that you shall surely die" (2:37). What he actually said was "knowing you will know that dying you will die." In other words, "you will know without a shadow of doubt that you will die without a shadow of doubt!"

Shimei complied for three years, but then two of his servants ran away to Achish king of Gath, and Shimei went after them. As soon as Solomon found out what he had done, he apprehended Shimei and put him to death. No questions, no nonsense, he died on that very day!

How then did Adam and Eve escape immediate death (to anticipate a little)? The answer is that redemption stepped in to save them. There *was* a death on that very day; it was the death of the animal whose skin was used to clothe Adam and Eve. That animal died in their place. It represented Christ, the first of many thousands of sacrifices foreshadowing the death of Christ four thousand years later.

The creation of Eve: Genesis 2:18-25

So far everything has been "good" or "very good". Here, verse 18, we encounter something that is "not good". It was not good that the man was alone without a mate. This needed to be put to rights immediately, with the result that by the end of the day (the sixth day) everything was "very good".

As if to open his eyes to his need of a mate Adam is introduced to all the different "beasts of the field", that is domestic animals, and many varieties of birds to see what he would call them. So Adam gave appropriate names to all the cattle and other animals, and at the same time he would have noticed how contented they all were, each with its mate.

The time had now come for Eve to be created. God caused a deep sleep to fall on Adam, and while he slept He took one of his ribs and some of the flesh as well. Out of the bone He made Eve's bones, and out of the flesh He made her flesh. He did not simply make the woman (v.22), He *built* her, as the Hebrew says. She was to be a structure firm and durable, not the house-keeper but the house itself!

The woman is on the same level as the man: his rib or side. She is not his head to do his thinking, nor his foot to do his errands, nor his hand to do his work, but his side to go alongside him as partner and fellow traveller. Eve was taken from that part of man that protects his heart. Hence she was designed to protect her husband from danger and to receive his love and care in return.

This woman, verse 23

The man said, "This woman is now bone of my bones and flesh of my flesh; this woman he called Isshah (Woman) because from man (Iysh) was taken this woman."

Zo'th, this woman, is the first, last and middle words. As middle word it is the seventh from the beginning and the seventh from the end. Moreover, each half has 24 letters as if to remind us that man and woman have both twelve pairs of ribs and are therefore well matched.

The words Iysh and Isshah sound alike. Isshah is derived from a root meaning to be weak. Iysh may be derived from a different root, but that is uncertain. Men may imagine they are stronger than women, but that is not usually the case. Women are often stronger than men morally and even physically since they are the ones who live longer!

Both Adam and Eve were naked (*'arummim*), but they were not ashamed. Nakedness was a token of their innocence, a sure sign of their moral purity before the Fall.

Genesis 3:1-24

The crafty serpent: Genesis 3:1

The serpent is described as "more crafty (wise or shrewd) than other beasts of the field." It was therefore a beast of the field like other domesticated animals to be found in the Garden of Eden (2:19; 3:14).

The word translated "crafty" can have a negative meaning (e.g. twice in Job), but more often it is positive. The serpent was the way God had created it, and shrewdness was its distinctive characteristic. The word is found eight times in Proverbs in the sense of "prudent", in contrast to the simple or foolish. Here are a few examples:

8:5: "O simple ones, learn prudence; O fools, learn sense"
14:15 "The simple believes everything, but the prudent gives thought to his steps"
15:5 "A fool despises his father's instructions, but whoever heeds reproof is prudent"
22:3 "The prudent sees danger and hides himself, but the simple go on and suffer for it"

The serpent's prudence consisted in foreseeing danger and hiding himself. Other animals did the same but the serpent was better at it than the rest. This is where Eve failed: she pressed on imprudently and suffered for it. Our Lord advised His disciples to be "wise as serpents and innocent as doves" (Matthew 10:16). He must have had Genesis 3:1 in mind when He said that. He would not have advised His disciples to do anything crafty or crooked, so obviously crafty has a good sense in Genesis. It is all very well being innocent as a dove, but that on its own is not enough. Innocence needs to be tempered with wisdom. It is believers in particular who are often too trusting, innocent yes, but not wise. The result is they are easily tricked like Eve or conned by unscrupulous fraudsters. This is more true of today's world than any previous century.

Another thing, the word crafty or prudent is the same as the word "naked" in the previous word, namely *'arum.* This is obviously intentional. They are not the same word of course, but homonyms, two words that sound alike but have different meanings. Our own language is replete with homonyms, for example *raise* and *raze,* words that sound the same but have opposite meanings. We distinguish them by spelling them differently but that option does not exist in a phonetic language like Hebrew.

We find therefore "naked" and "shrewd" (or crafty) both expressed by the same letters, *'arum.* Nakedness in the case of Adam and Eve was a mark of innocence. We have therefore innocence and prudence juxtaposed in successive verses. Eve cannot be blamed for not being prudent, but she should have been suspicious when this serpent spoke, and rejected it out of hand when it contradicted God's command.

The temptation: Genesis 3:1-6

If the serpent was crafty in a good sense, the devil who spoke through it was crafty in the worst possible sense. He is obviously suspicious if not jealous of Adam. He saw Adam as a rival, someone who would usurp his place as ruler of the world (Matthew 4:9). This threat he was determined to nip in the blood. Adam must be destroyed at all costs, and he would do it through Eve.

First, he approached the woman on her own because he saw her as less resolute than her husband. Secondly, he pretended not to know what God had said. Eve had lived long enough to know that animals do not speak, she nevertheless talked with him as if this was quite normal.

Satan's question was a subtle one; it questioned what God had said: "Did God really say …? Eve should have run a mile and hidden herself, but instead she made the mistake of answering him.

Her answer implied that God was less generous and more severe than He really is. God had said *"every* tree of the garden"; Eve leaves out every. God had said nothing about not touching the tree; Eve makes this up. Eve's "lest you die" is less positive than "you shall surely die." Eve's answer was true in substance, but she was wavering and Satan knew it.

Satan sees his opportunity and seizes it. What he says is a flat contradiction of what God had said; "You will *not* surely die!" He implies that Eve will receive enlightenment ("your eyes will be opened"), and will become like God Himself knowing good and evil – if only she takes a bite from this fruit!

So Eve eats, and her husband who is now with her eats as well. Adam, we are told, was not deceived (1 Timothy 2:14). He did so with his eyes wide open in the hope of receiving knowledge of a divine and superior kind. They hoped to receive the *superior* knowledge of knowing good and evil, but the only knowledge they actually received was the *inferior* knowledge of knowing they were naked!

What they did next: Genesis 3:7

Their innocence was gone in a moment and they knew they were naked. So they sewed fig leaves together and made themselves loincloths. Walter Lewis Wilson in his *Dictionary of Bible Types* has this to say:

The fig tree produces beautiful, large, soft, velvety leaves which are very attractive and lovely to feel. Man's religion is quite like that. He knows he is not fit to stand in the presence of God, and so he manufactures a religious program and thinks that this will be sufficient. Fig leaves shrink very quickly and reduce in size to about one-fourth their original size. Thus they fail to hide the parts as they should. So it is with human religions. They are not sufficient to cover man's sin and need. Only the blood of Christ is sufficient as a covering that suffices the demands of God.

Adam and Eve prepare to meet their God: Genesis 3:8-13

Adam and Eve hear the sound of God approaching. Instead of running to meet Him as previously, they hide among the bushes. They knew that their situation had changed and they were afraid of confronting their Creator.

Called to answer for his disobedience Adam makes excuses and tries to shift the blame on to Eve and even God. "The woman whom *you* gave to be with me, she gave me fruit from the tree, and I ate." In other words, It was all your fault, God, for giving me this spineless woman. If it had not been for her it would never have happened. At least the woman tells the truth, "The serpent deceived me, and I ate."

Why was the temptation necessary?

Because, to do what God demands because one cannot do otherwise has no moral worth. The opportunity to do otherwise must present itself. Adam and Eve had the opportunity to prove themselves, but they chose instead to *dis*prove themselves. God was not taken by surprise of course. He knew how it would be and He had already formulated His contingency plan. That of course was the Lamb slain from the foundation of the world.

The serpent is cursed: Genesis 3:14

The serpent is cursed above all cattle and all beasts of the field. They too were cursed, but the serpent was cursed above them all. The serpent is told, "On your belly you shall go, and dust you shall eat all the days of your life." The serpent presumably had legs prior to this like other beasts of the field, but now its legs shrivel up to vanishing point, so that it has to move around on its belly.

Eating dust is both metaphorical and literal. In Micah 7:17 for example it is used metaphorically of the vanquished nations, "they shall lick the dust like the serpent, like the crawling things of the earth." See also Psalm 72:9 and Isaiah 49:23. But in Isaiah 65:25 it is literal: "The wolf and the lamb shall graze together; the lion shall eat straw like the ox, and dust shall be the serpent's food." It will not choose to eat dust, but unavoidably it will lick up the dust at the same time as eating insects and small animals crawling in the dust, or plants if it was still vegetarian.

Satan is addressed: Genesis 3:15

Verse 15 continues without a break. It is clear however that God's accusing finger has shifted from the serpent to the guilty angel who had used this animal as his mouthpiece. An irreversible enmity is fixed between Satan and the woman. Satan knows that his arch enemy and rival will be born of a woman, but he does not know which woman. So he hates all women and tries to corrupt them as he had already corrupted Eve.

Hatred is also fixed between Satan's offspring (lit. seed) and the woman's offspring (seed). The woman's offspring is Christ, and conversely Satan's offspring is Antichrist. But offspring is plural as well as singular. Paul says to the saints at Rome, "The God of peace will soon crush Satan under your feet" (Romans 16:20). Crushing Satan is primarily the work of Christ, but Christian believers are included among the woman's offspring and consequently they too will have a part in crushing Satan under their feet.

If the woman's seed include believers, Satan's seed include those who oppose Christ. Our Lord said to some of them, "You are of your father the devil, and your will is to do your father's desires. He was a murderer from the beginning, and has nothing to do with the truth, because there is no truth in him" (John 8:44).

It was not simply unbelieving Jews to whom Christ was speaking, but specifically "the Jews who had believed in him" (8:31). These were Jews who had previously believed in Him, but had now turned their backs on the truth and were plotting to kill Him. It is of such that the Hebrews epistle speaks when it says, "It is impossible, in the case of those who have once been enlightened, who have tasted the heavenly gift …. and then have fallen away to restore them again to repentance, since they are crucifying once again the Son of God to their own harm and holding him up to contempt" (Hebrews 6:4-6; 10:26-31).

Of all people these are the offspring of Satan in its collective sense.

Satan versus Christ: Genesis 3:15b

"He (Christ) shall bruise your head,
and you (Satan) shall bruise his heel."

It is the same verb in both lines and they must be translated in the same way. The ESV does at least do this unlike the NIV which has "crush" and then "strike". The only problem is that "bruise" is the wrong word. The correct translation is "crush", as in Romans 16:20 where this verse is referred to. Spurrell says in his *Notes on the Text of Genesis*, "The only meaning which can be philologically defended is 'crush'."

Satan did not go away rubbing his head and saying "Ow, that hurt!" Indeed not, he was potentially destroyed, as we read in Hebrews 2:14: "He (Christ) too shared in their humanity, so that by his death *he might destroy* him who holds the power of death, that is, the devil." Satan did his level best to destroy the Lord Jesus, but he only succeeded in destroying himself. He is now a doomed angel living on borrowed time, a convicted murderer on death row. If he has not been destroyed already it is only because he is useful to God as a rallying-point for all the wicked and disaffected among mankind.

To learn more of his fate we need only turn to Revelation 20:10, the last we hear of him. We read there that the

Devil, the Beast, and the False Prophet will be tormented day and night for ever and ever in the lake of fire. So is this what is meant by "crush" and "destroy"? All his hopes and fiendish plots will be crushed out of existence, and he himself will be destroyed ("made of none effect, reduced to inactivity", Vine).

The words "for ever and ever" (lit. "unto the ages of the ages") denote an indefinite period of time. His torment will be self-inflicted. He will torture himself day and night as he contemplates his catastrophic fall from grace, his appalling record and humiliating punishment. And in the end, fire destroys him (Ezekiel 28:18).

Eve and Adam are addressed: Genesis 3:16-19

Both Eve and Adam are condemned to *'itsavon*, pain and sorrow. Eve will have pain in bringing forth children, and Adam will have pain in tilling the ground and producing bread. The ground will henceforth be cursed and will bring forth thorns and thistles in abundance, assisted by rainfall which had not been seen before (2:5).

Moreover, because Eve acted independently without consulting Adam, her *desire* shall be for her husband and he will *rule* over her. The words desire and rule are the same as in 4:7 where Cain is told, "The sin-offering is crouching at the door. Its *desire* is for you and you will *rule* over it."

Eve's relationship to Adam has taken a plunge for the worse. Instead of being his equal and loving partner, she is now subservient to Adam, more like a sheep or cow than the help meet for him. There are some countries where this servile relationship still obtains, though hopefully not among Christians.

If there had been any doubt in the minds of Adam and Eve as to what dying involved, this doubt is now dispelled. "You are dust, and to dust you shall return." That is the stark reality – they were made of dust and one day they would return to dust. Nothing is said about resurrection at this stage. But Adam must have realised before long, if God did not expressly tell him, that he had not been redeemed from death simply to return to eternal oblivion when his life came to an end.

Eve is given her name: Genesis 3:20

The man called his wife *Hawwah*, Eve, "because she was the mother of all living (*hai*)." The two words are closely related. This clause must have been added later, since Adam would have said, "because she *will be* the mother of all living." Adam may have called her "Living" because miraculously she was still alive in spite of the dire warning that if she ate of the forbidden fruit she would surely die. This must have been an enormous relief to Adam, and a cause for prolonged thanksgiving. His wife was Alive, Halleluyah!

God made for them garments of skin: Genesis 3:21

The Lord is very gracious to the guilty pair. He does not simply impose pain and sorrow on them, He also clothes them with garments made from the skin of a slain animal. These were not simply crude leather trousers or jerkins, but *ketonoth*, princely garments with long sleeves and reaching to the ankles. The same word is used of Joseph's coat of many colours (Genesis 37) and the embroidered coats made for Aaron and his sons (Exodus 39:27). Tamar, David's daughter, was wearing a *ketoneth* when Amnon threw her out (2 Samuel 13:18), and Eliakim was clothed with Shebna's *ketoneth* when the latter was disgraced from being steward of the household (Isaiah 22:21).

That slain animal was a type of Christ, and we too are admonished to put on Christ. Paul says in Romans 13:14, "Put on (NIV, clothe yourselves with) the Lord Jesus Christ, and make no provision for the flesh, to gratify its desires", and in Galatians 3:27, "all of you who were baptised into Christ have clothed yourselves with Christ" (NIV).

These garments were made by the Lord Himself before Adam and Eve were expelled from the Garden. They were not sent out with nothing on, but smartly dressed in princely robes. Adam was still a prince, albeit a fallen one, and Eve a princess like Sarah. Their garments were suited to their station. The animals would have known who was boss and would have acted accordingly.

The Tree of Life: Genesis 3:22-24

Knowing good and evil was not the blessing Adam and Eve were expecting. It meant for them the loss of their pristine innocence and the actual experience of evil as well as good. There was no way they could be allowed to live for ever in their fallen condition. They were therefore shut off from eating the Tree of Life and expelled from the Garden for ever. They were actually driven out and re-entry was made impossible by the Cherubim and the flaming sword that flashed back and forth without stopping.

The Tree of life does however reappear in the Book of Revelation. The overcomers at Ephesus are promised that they will eat from the Tree of Life which is in the Paradise of God (2:7).

And this promise is fulfilled in Revelation 22:14 where the right to the Tree of Life and entry to the Heavenly Jerusalem are granted to the blessed ones who wash their robes. Conversely, those who take away from the words of the prophecy of this book will forfeit their share in the Tree of Life and the holy city (22:19).

At first sight there appears to be an avenue of trees of life on either side of the river in 22:2, but in fact these are not *the* tree of (the) life, which always has two the's, but simply living trees, or life-restoring trees, whose leaves are effective for healing the nations.

So ends the first episode in the history of mankind. The next episode records the first murder, and that more or less sums up the next six thousand years: murder, rape and pillage; wars, disease and death!

Appendix: The Numerics of Genesis 1:1

The first verse of Genesis is without question the most remarkable combination of seven words that has ever been written. Here we have God's stamp of authorship, His imprimatur, on the Bible as a whole. I refer to the numerical design underlying this verse. It is not my purpose to indulge my penchant for Bible Numerics at this time, but I cannot resist pointing out (for those who don't already know) the breath-taking numerical structure which stares one in the face when the Hebrew text of this verse is examined.

Hebrew and Greek are possibly the only two languages in existence that used their entire alphabets for numerical purposes on a systematic basis. The Romans used six letters, but Hebrew and Greek the whole lot. In each the first ten letters[2] correspond to 1 to 10, the next nine 20 to

---

[2] For example, alpha = 1; beta = 2; gamma = 3, and so on. Thus groups of letters can be looked upon either as a word or a number. For more on this see pages 110-115 of *The Bible! Myth or Message?* by Michael Penny

100, and the remainder 200 etc. The Hebrew sequence stops at 400, the Greek at 800.

Every number has its own special significance in Bible Numerics, the two most important being 7 and 37. These two numbers are imprinted on Genesis 1:1 to an extent which can only be called miraculous. They speak of Perfection and the Word of God, both of which are highly prominent in this opening chapter of the Bible. Numerical design runs right through the Bible (and the whole of God's creation for that matter), but these two numbers appear far more frequently in Genesis One, and especially 1:1, than anywhere else that I am aware of. Here are a few examples from the first verse:-

There are 7 words, 28 letters
The first three words ("In the beginning God"), 14 letters
The last 4 words,14 letters
Fourth and fifth words ("the heavens"), 7 letters
Sixth and seventh words ("and the earth"), 7 letters

Numerical Value (NV) of the whole of Genesis 1:1 is 2701, that is 37 x 73

The first five words ("In the beginning God created the heavens"), 1998, 37 x 54
The last two words ("and the earth"), 703, 37 x 19
First and third words ("In the beginning God"), 999, 37 x

27

Second, fourth and fifth words ("created the heavens"), 999, 37 x 27

The sixth word ("and"), 407, 37 x 11

The seventh word ("the earth"), 296, 37 x 8

The three nouns (God, the heavens, the earth), 777, 37 x 21

God, the heavens, 481, 37 x 13

Note also the following:-

"And the Spirit of God moved on the face of the waters", 1369, 37 x 37

"And God said, Let there be light, and there was light. And God saw the light that it was good", 1776, 37 x 48 (2 x 888)

The third day as a whole, 15984, 37 x 432 (16 x 999)

"Let there be lights", 666, 37 x 18

"in the firmament of the heavens", 777, 37 x 21

"Let there be lights in the firmament of the heavens", 1443, 37 x 39

"And God blessed them saying", 1036, 37 x 7 x 4

"And God said", 343, 7 x 7 x 7

The written word cannot be separated from the incarnate Word. We are not surprised therefore to find the following:-

Iesous, Jesus, 888, 37 x 8 x 3
Christos, Christ, 1480, 37 x 8 x 5
Iesous Christos, 2368, 37 x 8 x 8
Huios tou anthropou, Son of Man, 2960, 37 x 8 x 10

But why 37? I cannot do better than quote R.T. Naish from his book *Spiritual Arithmetic*:

The reason seems twofold. First, it is composed of 3, which speaks of Divine perfection, and 7, which speaks of Spiritual perfection, hence the number is admirably suited to express the Divine spiritual perfection of the Word of God. Secondly, the number 37 has a very remarkable mathematical property in that it unifies the product whenever it is multiplied by 3 or any multiple of 3 up to the third power. Thus 3 times 37 has the product of 111, 6 times 37 the product of 222, 9 times 37 the product of 333! It is the only number that has this faculty, and hence its peculiar appropriateness to typify the Word of God, for the written Word is the only Book that can bring real unity of heart to the different classes and races of mankind. It overleaps all barriers, and brings into closest bonds of fellowship by leading all to the Feet of the Living Word, the Lord Jesus Christ, so that they are 'all one in Christ Jesus'.

More on Genesis 1

Theories of Creation
By Sylvia Penny

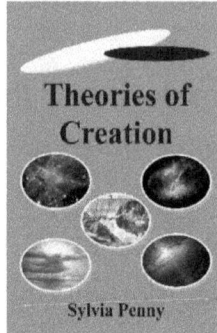

Creation is a fascinating subject! It is a subject about which there are many views or theories, in both the Christian and the scientific worlds, but which is the correct one?

In writing the book the author outlines a number of the theories put forward by different Christians. They are:

Biblical Interpretation	Scientific View
Non-literal	Theistic evolution
Day-age theory	Progressive creation
Six literal-days creation	Scientific creationism and a Young Earth
Gap theory	Ruin – six day reconstruction
Creation revealed in six days	No particular scientific view

Explanation is given as to how each interprets the account of creation as detailed in Genesis chapter 1. At the end of each explanation the advantages and disadvantages of each one are given dispassionately.

However, the aim of this book is to provide information about each view in an objective manner, so that readers can decide for themselves which one they favour. If further information is required on a particular theory, then the reader can refer to the bibliography included at the end of the book.

Copies of the book *Theories of Creation* can be
ordered from

The Open Bible Trust,
Fordland Mount, Upper Basildon,
Reading RG8 8LU, UK.

To pay by card, please order from **www.obt.org.uk**

*****

The book is also available as an eBook
from Amazon and Apple,
and as a KDP paperback from Amazon.

About the author

Charles Ozanne was born in Crowborough, Sussex, in 1936. He read Theology at Oxford before undertaking research in the book of Revelation for his PhD at the University of Manchester under F. F. Bruce. Sadly, he fell asleep in Christ in 2020.

He had submitted a study booklet to the Open Bible Trust entitled *The Essence of Ezekiel* but just before he died the Trust received an expanded manuscript entitle *Israel, Gog and Magog in Ezekiel*. Some of what is in this publication was also part of the earlier one. However, the OBT decided that we would publish it in memory of Charles as it is one of the last, if not the last, thing he wrote.

Charles Ozanne's Major Work

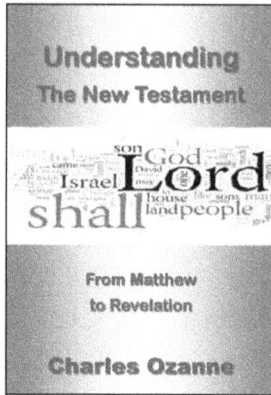

One of his major works is *Understanding the New Testament*, which is also available as an eBook. This is a well-written and well-presented commentary on the whole of the New Testament, showing that each of the 27 documents, although distinctive, fit into an overall pattern. For further details of this book, and his many others, please visit **www.obt.org.uk** (the Open Bible Trust website).

For details of the books on the next page please visit
www.obt.org.uk

Copies of the books can be ordered from

The Open Bible Trust,
Fordland Mount, Upper Basildon,
Reading RG8 8LU, UK.

To pay by card, please order from **www.obt.org.uk**

*****

These books are also available as eBooks
from Amazon and Apple,
and as KDP paperbacks from Amazon.

Books on the Prophets by Charles Ozanne

The Book of Immanuel (Isaiah 7-12)

The Essence of Ezekiel

Israel, Gog and Magog in Ezekiel

Empires of the End-Time: Daniel

The Fourth Gentile Kingdom (Daniel and Revelation)

Hosea: Prophet to Israel

The Day of the Locust: Joel and The Day of the Lord

Amos: The Lion has Roared

Who is like the Lord? The meaning of Micah

Nahum's Vision Concerning Nineveh

Malachi: The Lord's Messenger

Publications of The Open Bible Trust must be in accordance with its evangelical, fundamental and dispensational basis. However, beyond this minimum, writers are free to express whatever beliefs they may have as their own understanding, provided that the aim in so doing is to further the object of The Open Bible Trust. A copy of the doctrinal basis is available on **www.obt.org.uk** or from:

THE OPEN BIBLE TRUST
Fordland Mount, Upper Basildon,
Reading, RG8 8LU, UK